NIKKI ILES
Violin JAZZ IN AUTUMN
9 pieces for violin and piano

Contents

	Page
(Somewhere) Over the Rainbow	3
Hay Barn Blues	4
Autumn Leaves	6
Des Vendanges	8
Here's That Rainy Day	9
Danny Boy	11
Harvest Calypso	12
September in the Rain	14
Gypsy Waltz	16

CD track information is given at the top of each piece, in the form  **1**, 12, with the first (bold) number indicating the full performance track, and the second number the piano-only backing track.

MUSIC DEPARTMENT

OXFORD
UNIVERSITY PRESS

Arranger's note

I was delighted to be asked to continue this seasonal series for violin and piano and to have the pleasure of recording, once again, with the wonderful Ros Stephen. I am also grateful to Margrit Hasler for her invaluable contribution in the early stages of writing these pieces. Researching the various violinists who have shaped each genre has been enlightening for me and helped to bring a broad stylistic base to the collection on this theme of autumn.

The book takes you through a variety of musical styles from the Blue Grass of 'Hay Barn Blues' to the Cuban 'Des Vendanges' (grape harvest); and from the joyous swing of 'Autumn Leaves' to the rich harmonies of jazz classics such as '(Somewhere) Over The Rainbow' and 'Here's That Rainy Day'. The accompanying CD is provided to help you with the interpretation of the various styles—specifically the 'feel' of each piece. You will notice that Ros paraphrases the melody on the second time around the tune in 'Autumn Leaves' and also adds a few of her own 'slides' in 'Hay Barn Blues'. The notation here is just the starting point, so please, please feel free to interpret these arrangements in your own way!

OXFORD
UNIVERSITY PRESS

Great Clarendon Street, Oxford OX2 6DP,
United Kingdom

Oxford University Press is a department of the University of Oxford.
It furthers the University's aim of excellence in research, scholarship,
and education by publishing worldwide. Oxford is a registered trade mark of
Oxford University Press in the UK and in certain other countries

This collection © Oxford University Press 2016

Nikki Iles has asserted her right under the Copyright, Designs
and Patents Act, 1988, to be identified as the Author of these Works

First published 2016

ISBN 978-0-19-340767-1

Music origination by Katie Johnson

Printed in Great Britain on acid-free paper by
Halstan & Co. Ltd, Amersham, Bucks.

Credits
Cover illustration by Tony Stephenson © Oxford University Press
Artist photo by Hugh Byrne

The *Violin Jazz in Autumn* CD was recorded at Red Gables Facilities,
Greenford, on 28 April 2016. Engineered, co-produced, and edited
by Ken Blair, BMP The Sound Recording Company Ltd.

(Somewhere) Over the Rainbow

words by E. Y. HARBURG
music by HAROLD ARLEN
arr. Nikki Iles

inspired by Mark Feldman

Hay Barn Blues

NIKKI ILES

inspired by Big Bill Broonzy

Autumn Leaves

words by JACQUES PRÉVERT

music by JOSEPH KOSMA

arr. Nikki Iles

Bright swing (♩♩ = ♩³♪) ♩ = 144

optionally embellish rhythm on repeat

to Coda

D.S. al Coda

CODA

in your own time

inspired by Didier Lockwood

Des Vendanges

NIKKI ILES

Nikki Iles

Violin

Jazz in Autumn

Piano accompaniment book

Contents

	Page
(Somewhere) Over the Rainbow	2
Hay Barn Blues	6
Autumn Leaves	10
Des Vendanges	15
Here's That Rainy Day	20
Danny Boy	25
Harvest Calypso	28
September in the Rain	31
Gypsy Waltz	36

MUSIC DEPARTMENT

OXFORD

UNIVERSITY PRESS

(Somewhere) Over the Rainbow

words by E. Y. HARBURG
music by HAROLD ARLEN
arr. Nikki Iles

Expressively ♩ = 60

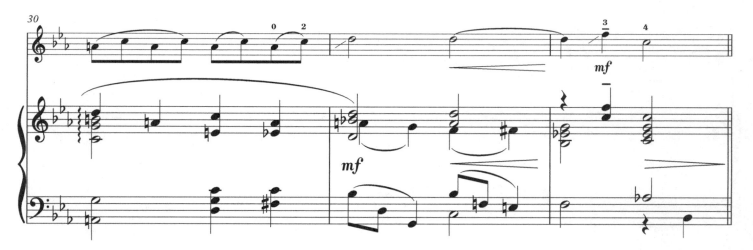

inspired by Mark Feldman

Hay Barn Blues

NIKKI ILES

Slow blues (♩♩ = ♪♪) ♩ = 76

inspired by Big Bill Broonzy

Autumn Leaves

words by JACQUES PRÉVERT
music by JOSEPH KOSMA
arr. Nikki Iles

to Coda ⊕

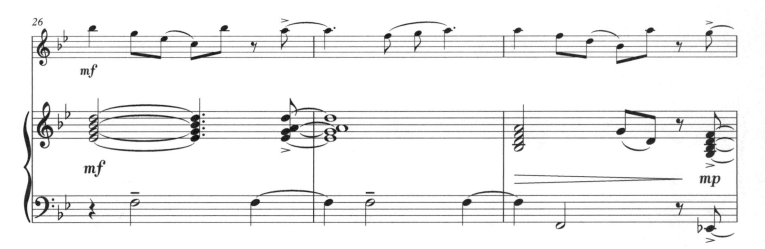

D.S. al Coda

CODA

rall.

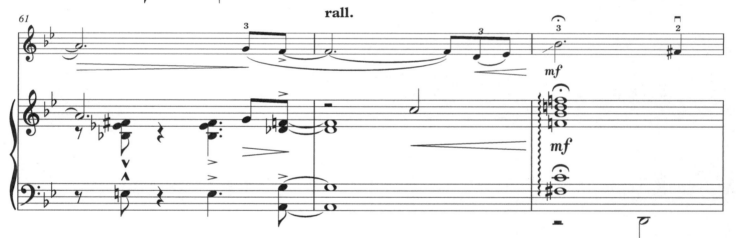

in your own time

inspired by Didier Lockwood

Des Vendanges

NIKKI ILES

Freely, with flamboyance

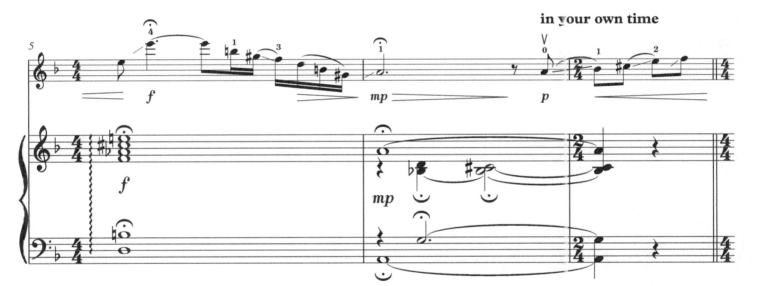

Gentle Cuban ♩ = 104

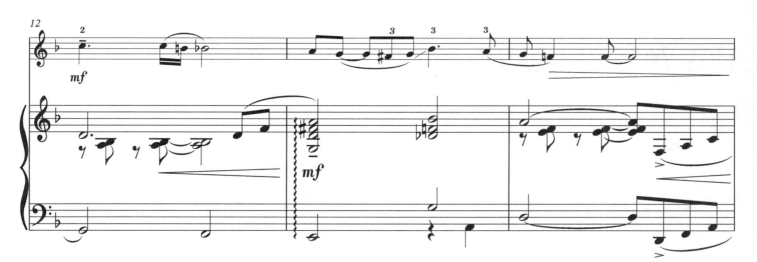

slightly pull back   **a tempo**

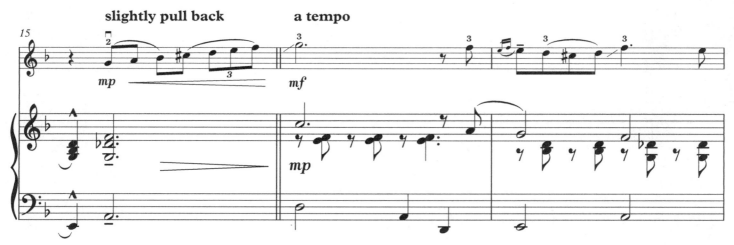

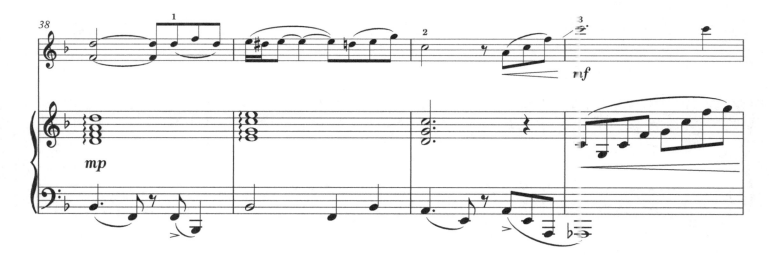

Intensely

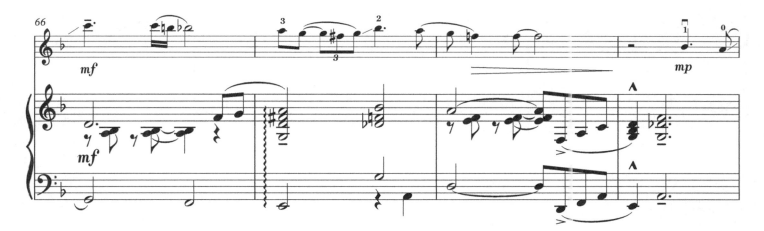

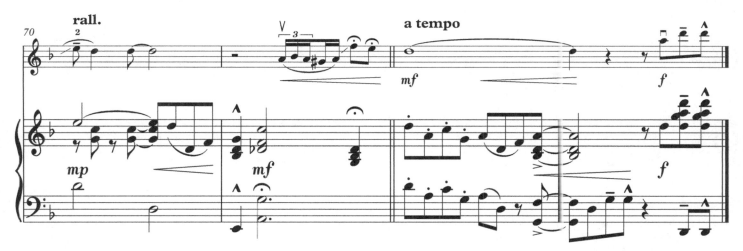

inspired by Omar Puente

Here's That Rainy Day

words by JOHNNY BURKE
music by JIMMY VAN HEUSEN
arr. Nikki Iles

Gentle, understated bossa nova ♩ = 108

Intensely

Broadly   **rall.**

a tempo

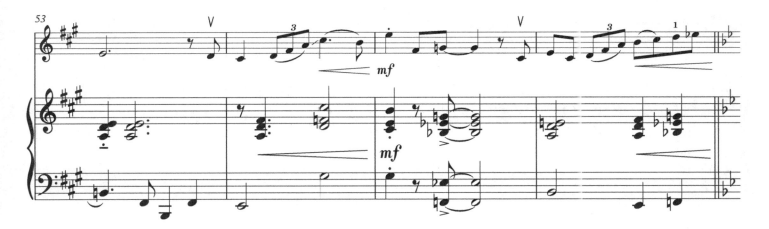

opt. 8va (until b. 63)

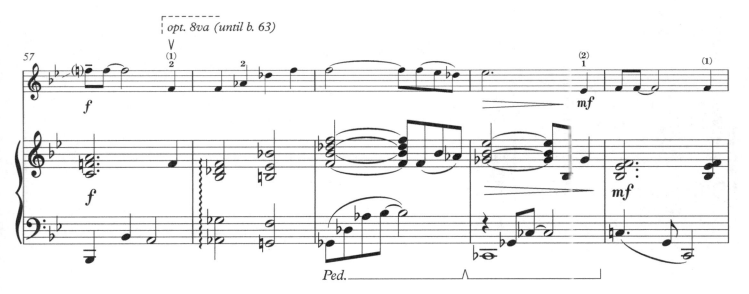

Ped.

inspired by Chris Garrick

Danny Boy

trad. Irish
arr. Nikki Iles

Freely, with expression

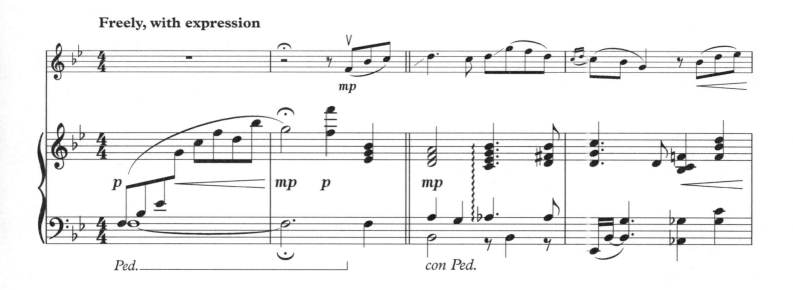

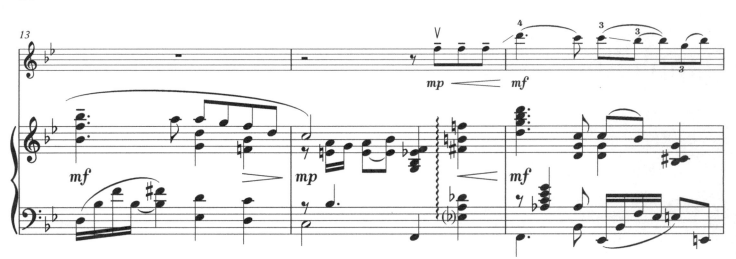

inspired by Yehudi Menuhin

Harvest Calypso

NIKKI ILES

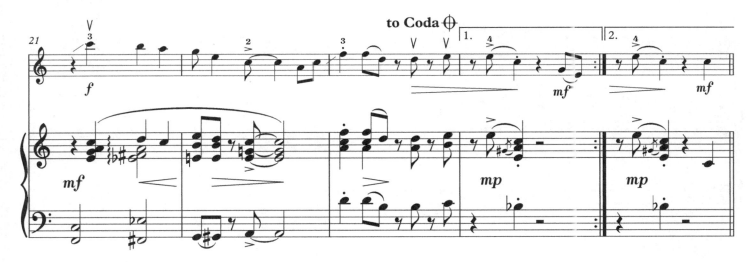

D.S. al Coda
(take 2nd endings)

CODA

inspired by Regina Carter

September in the Rain

words by AL DUBIN
music by HARRY WARREN
arr. Nikki Iles

D.S. al Coda

CODA

rall.   in your own time

inspired by the George Shearing Quintet

Gypsy Waltz

trad.
arr. Nikki Iles

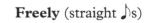

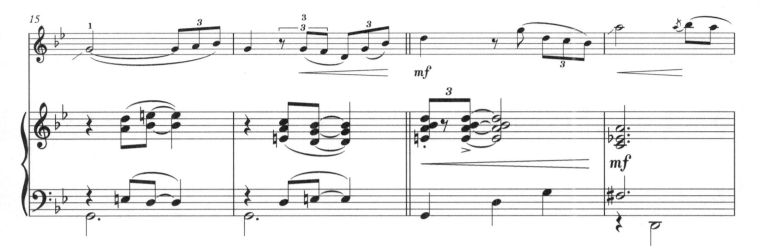

opt. 8va (until b. 24)

inspired by Stéphane Grappelli

inspired by Omar Puente

tracks **5**, 14

Here's That Rainy Day

words by JOHNNY BURKE

music by JIMMY VAN HEUSEN

arr. Nikki Iles

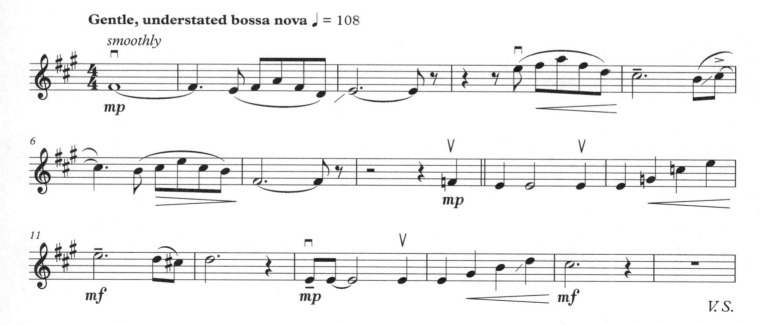

V. S.

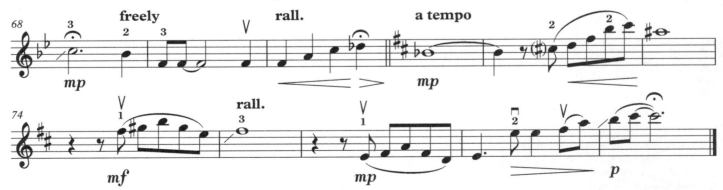

inspired by Chris Garrick

Danny Boy

trad. Irish
arr. Nikki Iles

inspired by Yehudi Menuhin

Harvest Calypso

NIKKI ILES

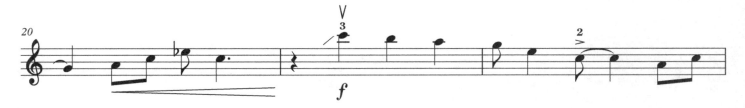

D.S. al Coda
(*take 2nd endings*)

inspired by Regina Carter

September in the Rain

words by AL DUBIN
music by HARRY WARREN
arr. Nikki Iles

D.S. al Coda   **CODA**

rall.   in your own time

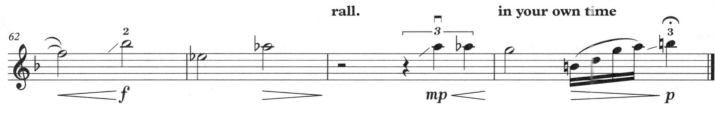

inspired by the George Shearing Quintet

Gypsy Waltz

trad.

arr. Nikki Iles

inspired by Stéphane Grappelli